In the Black Window

in the black window

NEW AND SELECTED POEMS

Michael Van Walleghen

UNIVERSITY OF ILLINOIS PRESS

URBANA AND CHICAGO

© 2004 by Michael Van Walleghen
All rights reserved
Manufactured in the United States of America
1 2 3 4 5 C P 5 4 3 2 1

♾ This book is printed on acid-free paper.

Library of Congress Cataloging-in-Publication Data
Van Walleghen, Michael, 1938–
In the black window : new and selected poems /
Michael Van Walleghen.
p. cm.
ISBN 0-252-02921-6 (cloth : acid-free paper)
ISBN 0-252-07178-6 (pbk. : acid-free paper)
I. Title.
PS3572.A54515   2004
811'.54—dc22   2003021631

Acknowledgments

Grateful acknowledgment is made to the following publishers
and editors of the journals in which the poems in this book were
originally printed or collected:

The University of Illinois Press for poems from *The Wichita
Poems* (1975), *More Trouble with the Obvious* (1981), and
Blue Tango (1989)
The University of Pittsburgh Press for "Clarity," "The Elephant
in Winter," "Periscope," "Beauty," "Twilight of the
Neanderthals," "Ghost," "Shangri-La," "In the Company of
Manatees," and "The Last Neanderthal" from *The Last
Neanderthal,* © 1999. Reprinted by permission of the
University of Pittsburgh Press.
The University of Pittsburgh Press for "Adios Zarathustra,"
"The Awards Banquet," "In the Chariot Drawn by Dragons,"
"Crawlspace," "Late," "Tall Birds Stalking," and
"Uncomfortable Procedures" from *Tall Birds Stalking,*
© 1994. Reprinted by permission of the University of
Pittsburgh Press.
Black Warrior Review for "The Former Life" and "Orchids"
Crazy Horse for "The Man in the Diving Suit"
Field for "When . . ."
Gettysburg Review for "Fidelity"
Hudson Review for "Coyote" and "Happiness"
Kenyon Review for "The Ex"
Margie for "The Franz Kafka Fellowship Hotel"
Southern Review for "Once More with Mother on the Beach"
and "Taps"
Willow Springs for "Ego"

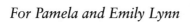

For Pamela and Emily Lynn

Contents

New Poems (2003)

FIDELITY

When they open the door
of their new Dodge Caravan
and the dog gets loose

it's 3:30 and 33 degrees
in yellow, foot-high numerals

on the digital clock
just inside the Fidelity
Savings and Loan parking lot.

It's also snowing a little . . .
not much, but enough apparently

to undo some woman in a BMW
who, as she hits the dog, screams
then puts her hand to her mouth

in horror—but doesn't stop.
It's 3:31. A flagpole

rattles in the wind somewhere
while the child whose pet it was

a girl about twelve or so
limps around the parking lot
in squeaking, wordless circles—

a tiny, intricate cog right now
whose turning turns the earth
as it circumnavigates the sun

until the great, clockwork wheel
of the synchronous galaxy itself

ticks forward on its axis
making it 3:32, and suddenly
her mother can touch her again.

I'm the man across the street
buying a newspaper at the 7-Eleven.

And there's someone else, a clerk
or teller from the loan company
who's come out in his shirtsleeves

like an angel of The Repossession
to cover the dog with a rug . . .

Meanwhile, cars and trucks
are speeding by, a few
stray flakes of snow

fall down melting in my hair
and life goes on, as they say

whether we pay attention or not.
Prince? Ralph? I'm almost sure
she yelled his name out once

but I've forgotten it already.
As if I *should* remember it . . .

as if, at 3:33 by the bedside clock
I'd just woke up again, haunted
by a name that won't come back—

some long-dead classmate maybe
or a lost girlfriend. Right now

it's a German shepherd I think—
gray for the most part, but darker
at the muzzle, ears, and feet.

TAPS

The sun is almost down
and except for the woman
dressed in white,
              shading

her eyes
       with one hand
waving with the other,
the far shore
         of Whitefish Lake
has turned an otherworldly
deep autumnal yellow . . .

I am in a boat
         with my best friend
who is learning
how to play the trumpet—

a cracked
       and off-key "Taps"
the only piece he knows . . .

But just wait.

Beyond the trees somewhere
and beyond
            their bright reflections
in the Lethean
            leaf-strewn water
one can almost hear
                        those same
few notes returning . . .

but clear
            and bell-like now
as if perfected
            in childhood's dark
unechoing wood
                        by such desire
even the distant
                        cold iron clang
of drunken
            loudmouth horseshoes
becomes
            a kind of metronome

and my best friend's name
called out
            to call him in
for supper
            seems at once
no more
            than who he is

and a cry
           that's wholly other—
foreign
           as Chinese somehow

yet in a key
           that's still
familiar,
           one of those
two-note
           descant replies
I've unaccountably remembered
from some Gregorian
                        choir-boy
chant for the dead . . .

but now,
           right now
we don't know
           what happens next—

the cancer
           just beginning
in his mother's breast
is only as big
           this fall
as the head of a pin

on which the wincing
                        listening angels
are carefully
           carefully dancing.

8

THE EX

In trailer parks
in Laundromats

in the smoke and mirrors
of trying to raise a kid

and dance her topless way
through business school

at Don Juan's, Pop-a-Tops,
the Houston Inn, the years

like disremembered years
she might indeed have spent

in prison, blur by outlived
until she somehow graduates

finds a decent job for once
then buys the run-down house

across the street—where now
shuffling back and forth

or stumbling, in her moonlit
gravel driveway, a tall

bare-chested skinny guy
scribbled hieroglyphically

over with homemade hearts
daggers, drops of blood

is shouting, beer in hand
that all he wants *goddamnit*

is to see his kid again . . .
but here come the cops

just like in the old days
with their blinding lights

and handcuffs instead. Now
they'll want to talk to her

too, they'll want to know
everything, the whole story

and then, God help us Jesus
the kid will want to know . . .

But first, there's the next
few minutes to get through

and her old name to remember
while they try their level best

to beat his idiot brains out
for kicking in a headlight.

Of course. What else is new?
Nothing in this life certainly

and nothing in that squawk
and static hissing either

from the police car radio
that couldn't just as well

be noise from some dim star
beyond the far Crab Nebula

where she got married once.
She understands that much.

And as anyone watching
from their lawn or porch

can see, the rest of it
is slowly coming back—

along with that funny name . . .
oh, right there, on the tip

of her tongue! It sounds
like a club clubbing meat

and rhymes with something
close to death I think.

COYOTE

I could tell
        from the briskness
of her stride
          and the level
steadfast focus
          of her gaze
that she was on a mission
of some importance . . .

but so was I
        that 4:00 A.M.
and towing a boat besides—
speeding on my dim,
           lost way
to some unpronounceable lake
in southern Illinois
I'd never fished before.

Otherwise,
        because her numinous
and fleeting disregard
          seemed almost
apparitional,
        I think I might
have turned the car around

and tried to follow her
with my headlights
                    for a while
just to see
            if she was real.

And then,
            as birds start up
and formless night,
                    beyond
the car's black windows,
                            gives way
to light again,
            I find the turnoff
I thought
            I'd missed somehow . . .

a road
        that turns past fields
of milkweed,
                ruined orchards
and collapsing barns—

beside which,
                constellations
of entropic
            farm machinery
rust half-visible
through their nebular fog.

And no one anywhere.
                    No cars.
No signs along the road.
                    As if
whoever lived here once
had vanished
                    unaccountably—

like one of those flawed
and mythic civilizations
                    lost
in blear antiquity,
                    wiped out
by plague
            or put to the sword
by some barbarian army . . .

But even as the catastrophe
is upon them,
                    the goddess Artemis
sets off
        at the speed of light
to petition Zeus,
                    who lives
far from here,
                    far from here
at the end of the universe . . .

or in the next county
where she appears,
                    in her dawn-gray
numinous guise,
                    as coyote—

and quite as real
                    as you
or I—
          slamming on the brakes
for wild-eyed,
                    well-antlered
Actaeon,
          chased by dogs
and leaping out of nowhere

three feet
          in front of the car.

ORCHIDS

By the time
           we'd transferred
from subway to bus

on the way to the zoo
and botanical gardens
in the unfamiliar city

the sun was out again—
March-bright,
                glittering
in the just-stopped rain . . .

to the point of blinding us
almost,
           especially as it caught
and dazzled
                here and there
on the broken glass
of weedy storefronts

and in the tiny
                trash-filled yards
of the ghetto poor.

I remember
        there was no one
on the bus but us—
                my wife
and me,
        our teenage daughter—
and no one either
              on the street . . .

a street
        that suddenly
a glimmering
            rag-stuffed window
or a chair-propped door
opening on a dark hallway
made eerily familiar . . .

images
        I recognized somehow
from my childhood
             in Detroit
nearly fifty years ago.

I was with my mother
and we were going
            to the aquarium
and botanical gardens
            on Belle Isle.

And this
        would be the neighborhood
near the river
            off Jefferson Avenue
where she grew up—
                but different now,
run down,
        the old house
by this time
        gone completely.

I must have been
            six or seven
and had never seen houses
like that before,
            houses
that looked
        as if they'd been
on fire—
        and weed-choked yards
with mattresses in them,
old stoves,
        couches . . .

Meanwhile,
        we've turned a corner
and abruptly
        there are trees again
and the houses
        all get bigger—
some of them with stone
or wrought-iron fences.

And then
        a high stone wall
that opens finally
on the botanical gardens—
where there are people
                    everywhere
studying their maps,
                deciding
what to see,
        where to go exactly.

We're here
        to see the orchid show—
to walk with the crowds
through the wet,
                glittering
arboretum,
            admiring the exotic
three-petaled bloom
                of flowers

I can first remember seeing
with my mother
            all that long
long time ago—
            their intricate
labiate mouths still whispering
of that first garden
                I'd learned about
at school,
        along with the angel
and his fiery sword.

ONCE MORE WITH MOTHER
ON THE BEACH

Florida, 1997

Is that seagull limping?
my mother asks,
              handing me
the binoculars.
              Listen . . .
I think it's crying for help.

Sciatic,
       all but deaf
these days
         and bothered now
with cataracts,
           she thinks
it has a mate out there—

male
      of course
            and entirely
impervious,
        a feckless dot
she can't quite focus
just beyond the breakers.

But his erstwhile wife
looks fine to me,
                    healthy
in her zoom-close proximity
to the point of corpulence
almost,
          and in glad possession
of a large,
              dead fish—

a narrative turn
                    at once
so dissonant,
                so thoroughly
familiar,
          it makes us stop
and laugh out loud . . .

before we start again
on living wills,
                  my brother's
suicide,
          and why it is
I see her
          only once a year.

Meanwhile,
              a puttering flag
on the lifeguard tower

accelerates
        like some kind
of puny,
     relic biplane
          taking off
in fifty knots of wind—

and all around us,
         above
each ebb-tide wave,
          sandpipers
tack
   and hover,
       tack
        and hover

but still can't land,
         blowing
leeward past us finally
like little,
     peeping scraps
of torn-loose seafoam . . .

Even the expensive yacht
I can barely see,
        plunging
desperately
     along the horizon
seems lost
      and going nowhere . . .

Look at that!
           I shout
handing back the binoculars—
That boat's in trouble!

But my mother
                doesn't see it,
focusing instead
                on something else—

that wayward bird again
or perhaps
                some tiny
drop of mist,
                a speck
so far from any resolution
it might have been
                my father.

THREE-RING CIRCUS

Venice, Florida, February 2003

The bridge is up
and we're stuck here

for a while, two minutes
or so, while a curiously

tublike little sailboat—
a renovated crab boat maybe—

chugs importantly by
below us toward the gulf . . .

my two old aunts agreeing
meanwhile, back and forth

from the hot backseat,
how curiously un-Detroit

it was to drive down here—
bumper to bumper everywhere

*and a silly boat like that
stopping all this traffic!*

Pelicans, bells going off . . .
a regular *three-ring circus*—

which, apropos of Venice
Ringling's winter home

for clowns, acrobats
and animal acts alike

rings yet another bell—
oh, another bell entirely

as the drawbridge shuts
and we start to move again

with our candy and flowers
toward Venice Hospital

where, by my watch at least
it's long past lunch already

and only ten minutes or so
before walking practice . . .

a nurse holding my mother
by a strap as she shuffles

her stroke-wobbly shuffle
at just about five feet

per minute down the hall—
much like a bear I think

learning how to ride a bike
or a runaway teenage acrobat

maybe, learning how to fly . . .
her bored partner hanging

from his knees somewhere
at the top of the big top

like a huge, shadowy bat
or, at three in the morning

like a television somehow
on which a clumsy boat

keeps chugging out to sea
under the uplifted bridge

that separates this world
from the astonishing next.

WHEN . . .

When,
        this middle March
at 6:00 A.M.
                the frozen shadow
of the still
            unbudded lilac
first appears
            then darkens
like an X ray
            limb by limb
on that senile
            stroke-seized face
two black windows
                and a door
might seem
        to likewise make
from Mrs. Merkle's
                falling down
one-car garage,
                it must be time.

Precisely
        time in fact—

as in some cosmically
                coordinated
Aztec ritual perhaps . . .

wherein,
        once more,
                at the coincidence
of true dawn
        and the equinox

one of the ancient ones,
                        one
of the grandmothers,
                is chosen.

And then,
        her nervous
                half-blind
oldest daughter,
                arriving
in a blurred sedan
                of blue feathers
for all her mother knows

climbs the steep
                pyramid steps
and rings
        the ceremonial bell . . .

Whereupon,
        they must both descend
of course,
        inch by shuffling inch
toward that selfsame
                feathery
blue sedan,
        and hence,
                the underworld . . .

which is somewhere
                    just south
of here I think,
                    a suburb I forget
a little east
                    of East St. Louis . . .

But once there
                    I would imagine
she will have
                    to surrender finally
her tiny,
                    two-ton vanity case—

a medicine bundle
                    she refuses now
to let her daughter
                    even touch . . .

full as it is
                    of all her earthly treasures—

spring mornings
                    that go all the way back
to kindergarten
                    with their feathery lilacs
and beautiful birds.

EGO

The lights come up
to reveal a large cage
in which lions and tigers

on various small perches
are uncomfortably sitting.

Yawns, a growl or two . . .
and then, after a while
through a little door

that squeaks half-comically
a man in jodhpurs appears

and bows to bored applause.
In his right hand, a whip.
In his left, a tiny gun . . .

Meanwhile, like a last breath
rattling in the dark somewhere

a feeble drum starts up
and starts the big cats down
all snarls and spit

to the fear-scented sawdust
where sits the teetery seesaw,

the ball they must mount
and roll with their feet . . .
likewise, the puttering bike

they'll ride on a leash
after jumping through hoops

of fur-singing fire. But why?
Why so terrified, so tractable
who fearlessly, fearlessly

for millions of years
stalked hominids like mice?

Couldn't they, if they wanted
tear this two-bit Mussolini
to shreds in a second?

Look at him, snapping his whip
shooting his little toy pistol . . .

It's hard to remember
this bustling, fat-assed
overgrown Boy Scout

bulging out of his clothes
once lived in a tree, never

dreaming a language like this—
which has a name, it seems
for everything. The lion

with the fierce black mane
is called Zeus for instance

and the female tiger is Kali—
who, for millions of years
fell upon us nameless

in the undulant grass
that had dreamt us all.

COELACANTH

In this morning's paper
two pages past Afghanistan

and opposite the story
of the kidnapped child

whose first-grade backpack
police have just recovered

from a rest-stop Dumpster,
there's a recent photograph

of coelacanth, a six-foot
female this time, fished-up

together with an amniotic
lump of her jumpy, unborn

pups, still alive in there
after 400,000,000 years

of floating room to room
through the mirror-confused

recursive, biocatacombs
of their dim, Devonian estate—

an area of vague latitude
somewhere south-southeast

of King-Kong Point apparently
in the moony bay of Madagascar . . .

where even now the bathysphere
of the mind's still alien eye

sinks downward once again
into the busy, finical abyss

of the downward-sinking diatom—
petals of a vast unblossoming

that fall and fall forever
back into the anaerobic muck

from which both withered Eden
and the fallen world began . . .

back when light-shy coelacanth
shrinking backward in her cave

was just a cyanotic pup herself
knee-high to absolutely nothing

and nearly half a billion years
from orphan-rich Afghanistan

or freezing East St. Louis even
where we'll learn tomorrow

they've found another shoe . . .
not a living fossil quite

but nonetheless a clue—buried
in the rest-stop, picnic snow.

THE OTHER SHOE

One minute I'm wearing
my go-to-hell white hat

exactly right, and the next . . .
After what? Two more drinks?

I'm falling off my first
sixty-five-foot barstool

in foggy, downtown Oakland
—then, being piggy-backed

still bleeding, Christ-like
from tough-guy wounds I hope,

back aboard the USS *Regulus*
AF 57, my brand-new home

where soon enough, the duty
chief bosun halts midsalute

to remind me with a quick
ham-fisted hook to the ear

that *Jesus Christ Almighty!*
I've lost a shoe somehow . . .

And one I'll lose again
in dreams of undiminished

anxious dread, once a month
or so, for over forty years . . .

Ah well. Never mind. Tomorrow
Japan! Or, more accurately

Alcatraz, the Golden Gate
and me again, throwing up

over almost everything aft
of my sea and anchor detail

sixty-five feet aloft, aloft
on the forward cargo mast—

a lily-pallored Billy Budd
yawing starboard to port

to lee back windward again
on his technicolored yardarm

but not quite dead just yet
—and no apotheosis either . . .

being merely the moron instead
everyone below is pointing to—

his crazily kicked off shoe
dropping down there forever.

LIGHT TAKES THE TREE

Man was created by the Trinity on the 23rd October
4004 B.C. at 9 o'clock in the morning.

> —Dr. John Lightfoot (1602–75), vice chancellor of
> Cambridge and master of St. Catherine's

Light takes the Tree; but who can tell us how?

> —Theodore Roethke, "The Waking"

It's precisely midnight,
October 23rd, 4004 B.C.E.

A lion somewhere. Hyenas . . .
while across the blue savanna

as far as the far Euphrates
God's first lightning trembles . . .

Beyond that, an intermittent
moon, of course: the terrified

and rolling eye right now
of some poor, chased beast

our feckless, dimwit parents
have yet to name so far . . .

Some kind of horse apparently
or bison maybe. But plunging

like nothing on this earth
from cloud to cloud up there—

the merest, mortal heartbeat
or collapsing grunt no doubt

ahead of God's fierce seraph
and his crackling, fiery sword . . .

Coming up, the long monsoon;
Abraham, and Jesus Christ

mixed with snow. Auschwitz.
Mankind, like celestial ants

crawling over the desiccate
dead-white eye of the moon . . .

Yet who but God himself
could ever bear to think

so far ahead? Right now
it's rosy dawn, 6:15

on the morning of the 24th
and Eve is six hours pregnant.

Blue skies above Mt. Ararat!
A lucky rainbow in the east!

While in the done-for garden
light takes the tree once more . . .

but who can tell them how—?
each bare branch glittering

with gems of unforbidden light—
as if the crystal dome of heaven

were all at once to shatter
and suddenly collapse for good.

THE FRANZ KAFKA
FELLOWSHIP HOTEL

Iowa City, 1963

I had this great fellowship
that no one in the graduate

admissions office seemed able
to remember quite. *Fellowship?*

Then why aren't you on our list?
But never mind. In a few weeks

or maybe months, depending
on when they found my file

they'd have the whole thing
straightened out completely.

Meanwhile, I had twenty bucks
and a room in transient city

right next to the bus station
that seemed to me, considering

the general drift of things
just perfect: lots of coughing

pine-scented fumigant, a rope
under the bed in case of fire . . .

which, given the peculiar logic
of my circumstance, ensured

as surely as it might in dreams
that a window I could barely open

opened on the close brick wall
I peed on every night—safer

in that rat-eyed, pervert dark
fire-trapped victim or not

than creeping down the hall
to the twenty-watt bathroom

that's for sure. The desk clerk
a little shy of four feet tall

seemed likewise perfect, almost
familiar—a kind of alcoholic

and strangely crippled friend
I may have beaten up on once

way back in the third grade
but couldn't place somehow . . .

our nightly, key-cage small talk
having always jumped by then

in a methamphetamine heartbeat
into even greater mysteries: flies

for instance, the way to stalk
and capture them bare-handed . . .

or now, a speechless contemplation
of his morbid index finger: *leprosy?*

which was his idea, or *gangrene*
which was mine. Who could tell?

And exactly here, it seemed apropos
that pipes should start to knock

an epileptic fall down the stairs
or, from a nearby room somewhere

someone's hacking cough spill over
into full tubercular hemorrhage—

as if, indeed, beyond all accident
I might have written it myself:

resonant, charged with meaning
but not precisely clear just yet . . .

being a mere rough draft so far—
the hard homework of my busy sleep

that long ago, invaluable semester
at the Franz Kafka Fellowship Hotel.

THE FORMER LIFE

It scatters and it gathers;
it advances and retires.

   —Heraclitus

On the great wheel
of birth and rebirth

at one momentous tick
turn, orbit or another

it's entirely possible
that some of us, most

of us, who could ever
guess how many, inherit

in the parsimonious interest
of a vast, metaphysical economy

and on condition of amnesia
the outworn, reborn soul

of someone else—some tiny
fierce Penelope, let's say

or, taking breath enraged
by all the same old noise

and stupid light, a squalling
infant Heraclitus maybe . . .

who must hence abide with us
anonymous and inaccessible

forever, a disposition merely
or merest inkling, intimations

that haunt us all our lives . . .
as when waking up sometimes

one hears again the surge
and rattling, long retreat

over small, loose stones
of the just-dreamt ocean—

a dream itself still haunted
by the fog-tripled clarity

of exuberant speech, birds
the measured, dactylic

splash of thudding oars . . .
POETRY! POETRY! What

dark poems had I lived
in the former life

and then forgot? I remember
by way of answer, the birdlike

shadow-writing of the leaves
against a sunlit bedroom wall

and how, despite the scattered
trembling incoherence there—

all that frantic self-erasure—
it seemed something nonetheless

that might, at any moment
gather into perfect sense . . .

if only for the tricky terms
for nightingale, dawn skies

those ocean dreams Penelope
left unraveled on her loom . . .

one right word or syllable—
some dim least letter even

from that difficult language
we'll all remember later.

TRANSFORMER

Gray, about the size
of a garbage can maybe

and situated on a pole
about twenty feet or so

above the backyard fence
it hums, just barely audible

day and night, years on end . . .
an incessant, one-note hymn

or hallelujah as it were
in nanosecond increments

to St. Jerome's precocious
fourth-century anticipation

of the dismal, second law
of thermodynamics: *Are you*

conscious of the stages
of your growth? Can you

fix the time when you became
a youth, an adult, an old man?

Every day we are changing.
Every day we are dying . . .

Or so, on this coincident
and frozen ides of March

while taking out the garbage
and listening to that entropic

anthem of the seeming air,
I've once more remembered it . . .

before finally noticing as well
the first spring robins, all

intensely listening themselves—
mesmerized, in fact, by phantom

echoes below the ice somewhere . . .
but wearing tiny helmets too

made entirely of snow, as if
by virtue of auspicious Mars

attendant at the equinox
remnants of a vanished legion

some on twig-stick crutches
were returned to us at last . . .

the way, perhaps, that childhood
itself—transformed by dreaming

day and night, years on end
returns to visit now and then—

our strange, immortal bodies
still taking out the garbage

but in a ratty bathrobe lately
and limping like a full adult.

FIXER-UPPER

The house across the street
is up for sale. Several people
a day pull into the driveway

cross the burned-up lawn
and stare into the windows . . .

They've redone the whole inside:
floors, woodwork, the three
marble fountains in the atrium . . .

All ten first-floor bedrooms
have either onyx or obsidian

hot tubs now—and however tasteless
one might think, an indoor-outdoor
Roman bath, carved entirely

from the bedrock granite, trumps
a dirt-floor basement every time.

But otherwise, the Monet lagoon
is mostly all filled in by now
and become a stray-cat jungle

of sumac, bug-riddled hollyhocks
and blackberry canes run wild.

And where are the tennis courts?
The ninety-foot, teak-wood yacht
they sailed each year to Greece?

The Turner-reminiscent sea itself
as a matter of fact? The one

one sees in all the magazines—
and photographed themselves
at dusk, from the backdoor

kitchen window. Let's look
inside again, hands cupping

our faces, so we can better see
what Van Gogh's worn-out boots
might have to say, their tongues

sampling the spilled litter box
under the white, formica table.

PERSIMMON FJORD

One midwest morning
in a sea-blink flash
of primordial sunlight

the school bus disappears
and a blue Camaro somehow
with dark, blue windows

parks thudding at the curb
instead . . . and when it sounds
for the third time or so

its three-note Viking horn
a Viking mother obviously—
operatic, larger than life

in her torn, white bathrobe—
comes banging out the unhinged
screened-in porch like someone

shoved suddenly onstage
at the last minute, breathless
and asked to sing an aria there . . .

before she spots in fact
the nose-pierced, tattooed lout
who used to be my paperboy

tumbling to the driveway
from a let-go drainpipe
and then just wrestles him

fucking this and fucking that
straight back into the house
then right back out again

of course, as if indeed
by way of old Norse custom
they might be dancing now

to celebrate his fifteenth year
and the first big cattle raid
of spring, the Icelandic

return of the walrus maybe
or the migrating narwhal . . .
and this, his first time

ever, to man the heavy oar
and hear all night—instead
of leafy-still Persimmon Street—

the monster-filled abyss
hiss and hiss, one scant inch
beneath his frozen ear.

THE MAN IN THE DIVING SUIT

A foggy morning
                sometime
in March,
          just before dawn . . .

He remembers
              the streetlights
were still on
               and thinking
as he ran,
            how they looked
at first
         like the blurry
light-filled portholes
                       of some
lost spaceship maybe . . .

and then,
           because it suddenly
seemed déjà vu,
                 lights from a boat
of some kind,
               viewed apprehensively
from the dark
               bottom
                       of the sea . . .

at which point
        the intricate
weedlike trees
        get poisonously
involved—
        porchlights,
              headlights
the reflective eyes
        of giant squid . . .

and clearly waiting,
        those blind
crustaceous-looking cars
        parked
end to end
        and still as stones
beside the scum-green lawn

where now
        he's on his knees
and gasping
        like a fish himself—
drowning there
        in his leaky
hose-entangled
        diving suit . . .

that through some trick
        of logic
he still can't fathom quite

becomes the same
                diaphanous
oxygen tent
              where he wakes up
baffled
        in intensive care . . .

his heart monitor
                beeping
beeping
      like unrequited sonar
through the abysmal deep.

HAPPINESS

Weep for what little things could make them glad.
   —Robert Frost, "Directive"

Melvin,
        the large collie
who lives in the red house
at the end of my daily run
is happy,
        happy to see me
even now,
        in February—
a month of low skies
and slowly melting snow.

His yard
        has turned almost
entirely to mud—
                but so what?

Today,
        as if to please me,
he has torn apart
                and scattered
everywhere
                a yellow plastic bucket
the color of forsythia
or daffodils . . .

And now,
in a transport
            of cross-eyed
muddy ecstasy,
            he has placed
his filthy two front paws
together
            on the top pipe
of his sagging cyclone fence—

drooling a little,
            his tail
wagging furiously,
            until finally,
as if I were God's angel himself—

fulgent,
        blinding,
            aflame
with news of the Resurrection,
I give him a biscuit
            instead.

Which is fine with Melvin—
who is wise,
            by whole epochs
of evolution,
            beyond his years.

Take
    what you can get,
that's his motto . . .

And really,
apropos of bliss,
                happiness
and the true rapture,
                        what saint
could tell us half as much?

Even as he drops
                back down
into the cold
                dog-shit muck
he'll have to live in
                every day
for weeks on end perhaps
unless it freezes . . .

whining now,
                dancing
nervously
                as I turn away
again,
        to leave him there

the same today
                as yesterday—

one of the truly wretched
of this earth
                whose happiness
is almost more
                than I can bear.

The Wichita Poems (1975)

THE LIGHT

On a cloudy day
on a day the clouds
the lake the late
small sun seem stopped
and the gray birds
dive like stones
or drift high
petrified and small
against the light
against that symbol, metaphor
and old analogy
to which the heart
perpetually aspires,
on such a day,
even Icarus
might have turned
and walked into the marsh,
noticed by tall birds stalking
and the glittering fishes
that, cloudlike,
move away.

A GOOD EXCUSE

It is snowing again.
A fine snow is sifting
over the broken fields.

There is nothing more
that you can do.
You need not think

again of moonlight
or of the several voices
which have called to you

like voices from the moon.
Where would they have you go
that is not the same

blank field? No, there is
nothing left for you
but to stand here

full of your own silence
which is itself a whiteness
and all the light you need.

THE PERMANENCE OF WITCHES

The moon
stars and weather
happen as they always have,
and between old Salem
where the pale women
burned like leaves
and this midwestern town,
the ash of dark reality
has sifted, settled down
and become the neighborhood
at suppertime,
the wives we take to bed.
And I think
those trivial lives
that gathered once
among the ferns,
among the oaks
that scattered near the sea
at Salem
were not more evil than our own,
but neither could the men
have better understood
what drives a woman
not to love.
Tonight, in black,
on a broomstick riding,
the witch the watcher
the spiteful other
coasts out and out

along the frigid edges of her life
and these abandoned shapes,
these faithful wives we love
and learn to hate,
this girl that moans
beneath me, far away,
this body burned
and sick to death
of burning, turns
in the pale half-light,
in the fires
hissing near the sea
at Salem.

THE ALLIGATORS

Feigning sleep,
to the casual eye
more dead than alive,
they wait. On them,
like a dinner plate
forever dropping,
all things depend.
One sees it clearly
in the eyes
of certain women.
After a time
not even their children
can pull them away.
I have seen them
standing tensely there
as at a window:
my mother
my grandmother looking out
one hand floating absently
among the dishes,
and the sink, the sink
soft-sucking things
it can't quite swallow.
I have seen them standing there
as rigidly as birds
who feel too late
the almost imperceptible
undulation of stagnant water.
When at last

they lift their heads
I've felt the whole zoo listen:
a neighborhood at dark
listening to streetcars
the far factories whistling
children, a lifetime
the perfectly indifferent
closing in.

FRANKENSTEIN'S 4:00 A.M. LAMENT; OR, THE MAN WHO LIVES DOWNSTAIRS

Yes, of course
I am a wretch,
stitched together
as I am, ill-made,
criss-crossed, a head
on someone's body, ears
on someone's head, a hand
that flutters up
from nowhere
like a dark wing
and murders the innocent
as they sleep, sleep
in their beds. No doubt
you've even seen me,
staring maniacally back
from rain-dark windows
or the bathroom mirror,
a face like death
warmed over, breathing,
the perfect likeness
of everything despised . . .
you know precisely
who I am. But listen,
can you hear me,
you, up there? I need
no less than you
forgiveness, love,
a place to stand—

yet even in this
my heart beats
like the clattering echo
of some kicked
and spinning chair
and already now
whatever it was
I was meant to say
becomes instead
a methodical shattering
of dishes, ashtrays, lamps,
a ripped-out telephone,
becomes as wrong
as someone screaming,
you, phoning the police,
and the littlest children
hiding in the hallway closet.

More Trouble with the Obvious
(1981)

MORE TROUBLE WITH THE OBVIOUS

A baby bird has fallen from its tree and lies feebly peeping dead center of the bright circle under our streetlight. What is there to do but bring it in? We dutifully prepare a shoebox, then mix up the baby food and hamburger of an old routine we know by heart, the ritual we've learned as children—but the truth is, in all the years since childhood, neither my wife nor I can remember having saved a single bird. We won't save this one either, trembling weakly now on the kitchen table, refusing to do so much as open its beak for our ridiculous food.

It lives with us two days, then dies suddenly in my hand—of "heart attack" my neighbor says. "Young birds like that almost always die of heart attack." He says this pounding nails in his porch and I believe him. In fact, I feel stupid for having mentioned it at all. A heart attack. Of course. The best thing would have been not to touch it. Perhaps it would have found a place to hide; and then, in the morning, its mother might have flown down to feed it. In any case, it's dead now and buried in the garden. The same garden, by the way, from which my neighbor's cat wrestled a live snake once into the hubbub of our barbecue.

But then I seem to have always had trouble with the obvious. Once, when a friend died, and after my parents had told me he had died, I came around the next morning anyway to call him out for school. His mother came to the door weeping and told me Orville couldn't go to school that day. I felt as if I had been walking in my sleep. I knew my parents hadn't lied, and I certainly knew what death meant; but somehow, until that moment, I must have thought it was just a dream I'd had. At school, another friend said he thought Orville died from eating donuts every night for supper. I had no trouble at all believing that. By then, donuts made about as much sense as anything.

A baby bird has fallen from its tree . . . someone you love perhaps is dying in another city. There must be something we can do. I remember one Sunday Orville and I got down on our knees in an alley and asked the Blessed Mother for a kite. When we found a rolled-up kite in the next ashcan with the rubber bands still on it, we *knew* it was a miracle. And we were glad, of course; but neither one of us, I think, was overwhelmed. We just believed in miracles and thought they happened all the time. We thought the birds we found needed milk and bread. We thought when they got big they would be our friends, do us wonderful favors, and keep us company forever.

CRABAPPLES

Somewhere in the Midwest
crabapples are falling

on a new Buick; crabapples
are littering the sidewalk

and a man is muttering darkly
to himself. It's not pleasant

to contemplate these crabapples.
Ordinarily he'd be having fun

oiling the doors of his Buick
in perfect silence. But not today.

No sir. Not with these crabapples
falling. Not with the driveway

looking like this. He oils up
and slams both Buick doors

then opens up his trunk
and removes a brand-new yellow

plastic garbage can. Perfect.
It's the perfect thing. Now

he must carefully cut up
his old plastic garbage can

and toss it piece by piece
into his new one. It's important

not to hurry and that each piece
be exactly four inches square.

It's important to do things right.
After all, he's got himself

a nice place there. Occasionally
a crabapple hits the roof

trunk or hood of his Buick
or bounces on the driveway

but basically it's a nice place
a good life. Crabapples, insomnia

tumors the size of someone's
little finger? That's nothing.

That's why he stays up past midnight
raking the driveway.

THE SIBYL AT SNUG HARBOR

The fish are biting
or they're not. Birds
wade the shallows here
in sunlight, or otherwise
appear for ghostly moments
in the fog, and the tides
move either in or out
the way they should
regardless of the weather,
for this is just Snug Harbor
where we fish. Today,
the perfectly ordinary sky
is blue, the windless bay
is blue, and the snowy egret
stalking minnows near the shore
seems somehow almost fake
and planted there,
like a lawn decoration,
the property of a Mrs. Garrison
walking over in hip boots,
her voice midwestern, flat out,
and friendly as the weather.

Yesterday, however, her husband
caught a strange fish here,
a fat eel or dogfish sort of thing
no one could identify. Disgusted,
they threw it back; whereupon
she was utterly amazed

to see it clumsily attacked
by an enormous seagull
who tried a full hour
to swallow it. Furthermore,
last night, she dreamt of it,
and her retired husband,
who has diabetes, arthritis,
and serious heart trouble,
was kept awake till dawn
by the sexual racket
of wandering, ferocious cats—
all of which goes nowhere, is apropos
of something she forgets . . .
"and in the morning"
her husband says, grabbing
at my arm, "the goddamn things
jump right out at you
from the garbage bin."

THE FISHERMAN

For nearly a month he had been having dreams in which he appeared to himself as someone he didn't like, someone he couldn't trust—and waking up he felt hysterical, dull, dishonest, and ashamed. But his wife thought that perhaps he had been working too hard and that maybe he ought to go fishing. He didn't particularly want to go fishing—he knew things were more serious than that—but the next morning before five o'clock he was dressed and driving toward the river.

He had been awake all night, and now, in his exhaustion, the river appeared a little too familiar, the hard clay path down to the water too predictably slick and dangerous. He was sure he had dreamt about this place. Perhaps he would sink into quicksand or miss his step and be swept away by the current. He can't remember now how it finally goes . . . but the path, certainly, seems something he remembers—also, the glittering cave of trees and the greasy, treacherous look of water bulging over stones.

Now he remembers he must throw a little wooden minnow along the edge of some fallen trees. The minnow is painted silver with terrified yellow eyes and he must throw it out over and over again, watching it return from deep water like something really alive, wounded, frantic, and pursued. He has dreamt this dream so often—himself pursued, himself the fisherman—he can hardly breathe. And then, when the fish hits, it's like waking up to a phone call he thought he'd answered already in his sleep.

The startled, headlong heaviness of the thing! But there's no question of ever landing it . . . only the heavy instant pulling him toward the dark before the line breaks—and afterward, the whole forest humming implacably as a dial tone after someone loved has just hung up. He sits down and can't believe it. He sits down like a man overwhelmed with mortgages, cracked foundations, and fallen gutters. And he can't believe the blue jay either, hopping toward him down the muddy bank like a mechanical toy—or that his wife is really seeing someone else.

THE HONEYMOON OF THE MUSE

*You're right. There's nothing
much to see out here but corn*

*and soybeans. Wake me up
when we get to Denver.* Yawning

this, the tired muse gives up
but Illinois goes on forever

with detours through Homer
Sadorus, Villa Grove . . .

towns nestled at the foot
of nothing—and therefore

precarious somehow, fitfully
alpine, as if the sky itself

might suddenly collapse
and wipe them out entirely.

*Are we there yet? Where's
the meadow, the hillside*

*the shepherd with his flute?
Let's stop and ask directions.*

Poor kid. She thinks Denver
is a kind of honeymoon resort

located high on the slopes
of Mount Parnassus. She thinks

I'm rich and the airplane roar
of my broken muffler means simply

that my car can also fly. Why
not? She can believe anything.

So here we are slowing down
for Villa Grove . . . two scarce blocks

of houses, body shops, and shattered
Chinese elms. No Denver certainly

but rare enough, a jewel really,
set high in the rugged mountains

of central Illinois. "Look . . ."
I whisper, kissing her perfect ear,

"there's a liquor store that's open
and a vacancy at the Villa Pines!"

WALKING THE BABY TO THE
LIQUOR STORE

It's nearly ten o'clock in the morning and I have work to do. I have to write a novel and a book of criticism. I have also a book of Mongolian double sestinas to translate, a verse play that needs a final act, and a movie script that's hardly off the ground. Besides that, I haven't published a book of my own poetry in weeks, so it's absolutely imperative that I get busy. But first, first I have to take the baby to the liquor store. A brilliant career is one thing—but being a good father, that's what *really* counts.

The baby adores going to the liquor store. In her infant mind there is, perhaps, nothing so beautiful or significant in this world as sitting up in her yellow stroller and rolling bravely west toward some exotically remote BUNNY'S—or, on Sundays, a place as unimaginably far away as KIRBY'S LIQUOR. Such, at least, is the radiant dignity of her expression. And when that snarling German Pinscher throws himself, all teeth and slather, against the pigeon lady's fence on Maple Street, she doesn't turn a hair. Why should she? This morning she's Cleopatra and the liquor store is Rome.

Believe me, I wouldn't miss these excursions for the world. I wouldn't miss them even if it meant giving up the National Book Award. How much trouble is it, after all, to go out walking with the baby? How much work could one possibly do in that brief half hour? And measured against such joy, such pure infant bliss (which may well indeed anticipate a lifetime's happiness), how important is it that I go to work at all? Sometimes, when we get home from the liquor store, the baby and I are so happy we even do the dishes and have a drink, by God, right there in the kitchen.

The baby knows four words: mommy, daddy, banana, and doggy. Could anyone write a novel more interesting than that? It's something I think about often in the glittering fluorescent kitchen after the baby's gone to sleep. And who knows what she'll come up with next? Luckily enough for me, the rigorous disciplines of my craft have trained me in patience. I can probably wait until tomorrow before going to the liquor store again. I can probably fall asleep on the porch tonight like any tired father in midcareer—watching the fireflies coming on and going out again in the long grass like so many sparks flying off the anvil of the world.

FUN AT CRYSTAL LAKE

After a day of whitecaps
and the threat of tornadoes
the lake turns calm again
a few mayflies begin to hatch
and by late afternoon even
the moon is visible.
                              Perhaps
things will work out after all.
Perhaps there will be fireworks
later on, or maybe a barbecue,
and if everyone behaves, maybe
a quick ride just before dark
in the speedboat!
                         I hope so.
I like happy endings sometimes
don't you? Take the kid
I caught just yesterday
for instance, at the beach
across the lake, stalking
a chipmunk with a brick.
                                    He was
"just having fun" he said
and that was that. No doubt
the people at the fancy lodge
are likewise having fun, especially
the man with the fireworks,
the motorcycle kids,
                              and whoever it is
who laughs so hysterically

after each explosion. In any case
what good does it do to worry?
What good did it ever do? Take
this dragonfly for instance
eating a bee
                on a red washcloth
or the man with the speedboat
yelling at his brainless son
again, for walking pigeon-toed
for having a sad face
an ugly lip, a forehead
like his mother's.

DRIVING INTO ENID

For Louis Jenkins

Hundreds of migrating hawks are roosting in the hedgerows around Enid, Oklahoma. If the sun were out you could see they were a reddish-brown and had creamy, speckled bellies. But today it's raining in Enid and the rain is mixed with snow. The hawks are merely silhouettes today, far off.

On sunny days, driving into Enid might easily remind you of a scene in a grade-school geography book: behind the hawk on the fencepost, a train goes speeding toward some grain elevators on the outskirts of the city . . . then the horizon, and an airplane flying low over a few tall buildings. But today the winter grasses tremble on the hillsides and the scarce trees tremble.

I was just thinking I had come a long way . . . I was just thinking that next year, for sure, I'd buy a new car. I must have been thinking something like that on the outskirts, passing the first small factories, the ragged fields strewn with junk . . .

Then, at the first stoplight, some kid waves at me from the backseat of a police car . . . inscrutable, fierce. He looks like a kid I knew in grade school. His mother wore a fur coat in the middle of summer and believed the Russians were shooting tornadoes at us.

What did he do? Where are they taking him? They found him in a culvert trying to gut a chicken with a piece of glass . . . they found him trying to build a fire out of cow shit and wet sticks. They found him all right and now he's going back.

Later on, I'll find his sister quite by accident selling cameras in the discount store. She has a crooked, shy face and reddish-brown hair. She's married now and her chewed fingers are tattooed SUE on one hand DAVE on the other.

ARIZONA MOVIES

1

Rosetta, her new boyfriend
and all four kids
are going to the drive-in
down in San Manuel.

"One more beer," they tell the kids
"and then we'll go." The kids
want a quarter a nickel
another dime—the kids

are a pain in the ass
the movie is about a dog
and the boyfriend wears glasses
baggy double-knit slacks

and a white belt. Rosetta,
on the other hand, is beautiful,
elegant, altogether sweet
in her new blue sweater

and when she reaches in her purse
to buy another round,
I spot her little silver gun.
"That's just in case," she says

"just in case."

2
Sometimes
even in the middle
of the year's best movie

you can hear coyotes
at the San Manuel Drive-in.

Tonight, they are far away
and merely barking at the moon . . .

but Rosetta tells me
that when they chorus close
and suddenly together

hysterical, high-pitched, furious

it means something is dying
in the dark foothills
behind the shaky screen.

3
After the bad movie
Rosetta wants to finish off
what's left of the tequila
drop off the kids

and then go dancing . . . !

But I don't know about Fred.
I think Fred sells mobile homes—
convenient, air-conditioned,
catastrophically fragile,

I pass them every day
and try to imagine myself
living there: the TV on
all the kids at school

and Rosetta just lying
on the couch, just watching
through the picture window,
some Apache ghost dance

cavalry of thunderheads
advancing slowly out
from between Mount Lemmon

and a pigeon-blue wing
of the Catalinas.

4
No one is dancing
up at Pop-a-Tops. No one
is speaking. The TV's on
and in the Merry Christmas

snow-flaked mirror, Fred
is shooting pool. Rosetta,
on the other hand, shreds
her matches into tiny bits

then looking up, her look
slides sidelong into mine—
the tense, unsteady look
I think, of children

getting lost . . . but what
was it that I thought to say?
Something dumb, mindless
a remark about the movie

or at my best, to notice
on that long, small arm
her careful, barroom bracelet
of pink and yellow straws.

Whatever it was, she answers
to the whole place—loud,
and before I say a word:
"Nope, I'm not dead yet"

and the fuzzed-up mirror
keeps still, stays quiet
as the slow blue echo
of a pistol shot.

5
Rosetta says she's 32
but Fred looks younger.
Fred's even younger partner
works the graveyard shift

at Magma Copper
and behind us all
the Falstaff clock
turns counterclockwise

toward eleven. "One more game,"
they tell Rosetta, "and then
we'll go." *The Lariat?*
The Hangman's Tree?

"Why not Rosetta's place?"
Fred's partner whispers.
A joke perhaps. But still
it's curious, frightening

that I should also hear
in the shy nylon whisper
of Rosetta's thighs
in the click of small ice

something dangerous, random
confused as kitchens,
cupboards where the knives
are kept, bedrooms

in the Apache Trailer Court
with real bullet holes
above the door.

6
Like Rosetta
I too hear voices.

Tonight, they are speaking
the frazzled language

of neon, the cindered
impossible language

of parking lots, static
and revolving lights . . .

but sometimes, it's Rosetta—
her voice still angry

clear, above the voices
of the graveyard shift

who slam their doors
like Fred or anyone

going off half-drunk
to work tonight

in knee-deep water
and the hot acidic dark

one full mile
underground.

Blue Tango (1989)

THE AGE OF REASON

Once, my father got invited
by an almost perfect stranger

a four-hundred-pound alcoholic
who bought the drinks all day

to go really flying sometime
sightseeing in his Piper Cub

and my father said *Perfect!*
Tomorrow was my birthday

I'd be seven years old, a chip
off the old daredevil himself

and we'd love to go flying.
We'd even bring a case of beer.

My father weighed two fifty
two seventy-five in those days

the beer weighed something,
the ice, the cooler. I weighed

practically nothing: forty-five
maybe fifty pounds at the most—

just enough to make me nervous.
Where were the parachutes? Who

was this guy? Then suddenly
there we were, lumbering

down a bumpy, too short runway
and headed for a fence . . .

Holy Shit! my father shouts
and that's it, all we need

by way of the miraculous
to lift us in a twinkling

over everything—fence, trees
and powerline. What a birthday!

We were really flying now . . .
We were probably high enough

to have another beer in fact,
high enough to see Belle Isle

the Waterworks, Packard's
and the Chrysler plant.

We could even see our own
bug-sized house down there

our own backyard, smaller
than a chewed-down thumbnail.

We wondered if my mother
was taking down the laundry

and if she'd wave . . . lightning
trembled in the thunderheads

above Belle Isle. Altitude:
2,500; air speed: one twenty

but the fuel gauge I noticed
quivered right on empty . . .

I'd reached the age of reason.
Our pilot lit a big cigar.

THE SPOILED CHILD

The spoiled child
sits quiet as a mouse

and learns to deserve
everything he gets.

It's Christmas Eve

so naturally his father
kicks the electric train

tracks, station, cars, and all
across the living room . . .

Next, he'll wrestle the goddamn
sonofabitch Christmas tree
right out of the house.

And furthermore, furthermore
if there's any more crying,
any more talking back

the spoiled child
is going to get it again
with the strap.

*

The spoiled child
is exhausted by all this

and lies down in his bed
like a dog. His sleep
is full of yips and moans

but he is not a dog. Not
at all. There's simply
been an accident of sorts

a train wreck it turns out—
wreckage scattered everywhere

shouts, the breaking of glass . . .

then the nightlong, high-pitched
whistling of the broken boiler

the cruel, absolute zero
of deep space, live steam
condensing into stars

galaxies, the permanent
blizzard of the universe.

*

Just before true dawn

still bright, still there
at this chill latitude

the star of Bethlehem
sits low on the horizon

appearing as a tiny moon
or some far light leaking

from a bedroom keyhole . . .

God has placed it there
beyond all accident
the spoiled child thinks

and beyond all accident
he hears the Herald Angels
singing each to each . . .

They sound like bitter wind
the cold labyrinth of home
creaking in the wind, dogs

the knocking of pipes
the ragged, high-pitched
snoring of the Magi

the fitful shepherds
even the drunken Minotaur

uncomfortable on the couch
in his human body.

THE AFTERLIFE

Because all of it happens
at the speed of light

the soul naturally lingers
curious, appalled I think

near the impetuous corpse . . .
and as for all that whispering

from beyond the bright doorway
let them wait. I remember

when I was about ten or so
hitting my head on the ice

then waking up in the hospital
anonymous and all attention

beside a dead man. The man
had a hole in his neck . . .

I could identify the windpipe
but various other things

were in the dark. His hand
was close to my hand, one foot

hung off the cart . . . Someone
a name that would come to me

had simply dumped him there
slumped in his tangled IVs

like a let-go puppet. He knew
precisely who I was. The logic

of his bloodshot, puppet eye
was inescapable. The windows

too, were inescapable, black
the coldest dream of winter . . .

All the rivers were frozen—
trashcans wandered in the street

like tumbleweed. A child's name
in fact, might wander years

without a coat out there
without a hat or even socks

and I tried not to think of him
huddled under the overpass

or sleeping in doorways
too cold to speak.

MEAT

It was early Saturday, dawn
the day for buying meat . . .

My father had this friend
way over in Hamtramck

who knew all about meat
and so we'd drive uxorious

drunk mornings after payday
halfway across Detroit

to meet this expert
at the slaughterhouse

where they sold everything:
brains, testicles, tripe

all the precious offal
grocery stores disdained—

whole hog heads for headcheese
fresh duck blood, fresh feet

kidneys, giblets, pancreas . . .
The freshest meat in the world

my father's friend would shout
above the squealing, bleating

foaming panic of the animals
and my father would repeat it

all day long. *The freshest
goddamn meat in the world*

he'd croon to the barmaids
along our long route home

forgetting, even as he said it
that all that lovely meat

was spoiling in the car.
But I remembered. I knew

the trouble we were in.
I could already see us

opening the bloody packages—
our poor brains, our testicles

smelling up the whole kitchen
again, and in the sorry face

of all my father's promises
to come home early, sober

a fine example for his son
a good husband for a change

one of those smart guys
who knew all about meat.

LAKE LIMBO

A cold drizzle
nearly every day
this week. The lake
green-gray, white-capped
the tiny beach littered
with oily dull debris
a wrack of Styrofoam
weeds and plastic rope
and where the water stops
a yellowish stiff froth
shivers and flies apart
all morning all day
in the steady gale . . .

Even the snot-beaked
seagulls look marooned
and stand blearily around
in little gangs, freezing

flat broke, unemployed . . .

                    *

Behind the scenes somewhere
a kid with a black eye
a figment of the weather
starts chopping down a tree.

He's been on vacation now
since 1948. His parents
are probably next door
playing cards, drinking gin . . .

Listening to the lake
I can hear the slap slap
of his dull ax murdering
every tree in Michigan.

I can hear him muttering
like a lost motorboat.
I can hear him snarling
like a troubled chain saw.

Self-loathing, rage
childhood without end . . .
these are calibrations
on an old barometer

in love with the abysmal.
The air is full of ghosts
voices, an ironic yodeling
as from the same two loons

that shamed me as a boy
chopping idly at trees
or killing birds up here
with my BB gun. Everything

seems precisely as it was:
childhood at its very worst—
a Tierra del Fuego of desire
on the brink of paradise.

BLUE TANGO

After stumbling around for months
like arthritic wooden puppets

unaccountably brain-damaged
and unable to count—failing

to fox-trot, failing to waltz
failing in the church basement

even to two-step correctly
it was decided we had danced

beyond all mere appearance
to some mystical new plateau

where henceforth we should learn
to tango. Our Dominican nuns

were adamant. The seventh grade
at the Assumption of Our Blessed

Virgin Mary School would tango!
The Saint Elizabeth Sodality

with whom we shared the basement
on Wednesday afternoons agreed.

They loved that music; it helped
them sew. That year, I remember

they were busy sewing things
the nuns called "cancer pads."

And when the long, elliptical orbit
of our tango brought us twirling

close to the glimmering windows
the flimsy tables where they sewed

I'd hear the whispered variations
of a single, incessant conversation:

By the time they opened him up
repeated someone, *it was everywhere.*

Then off I'd go again, mincing
with my awkward, too-tall partner

toward the gloomy furnace room.
Listening to those ladies talk

you'd think that suppurating cancers
had hit our parish like the plague.

Nor was there anything to do for it
but sewing cancer pads, communion

and learning, of course, to tango—
as if preparing for a long cruise

among the romantic blue islands
of the southern ocean. Some heaven

where even cabin boys could tango
and no one had to get up for work

at Packard's, Dodge Main, Cadillac . . .
where no one got pregnant, got cancer

lost their fingers in a punch press
or had even heard of Detroit, at all.

BOWLING ALLEY

There were six lanes
and a bar next door.

We worked two lanes
at a time. "Jumping"

it was called. Two
maybe three leagues

a night @ 13¢ a line
plus tips. It added up.

It was even kind of fun—
like being on a ship

and dodging broadsides
from the enemy. *Look*

lively lads! Right on.
You had to pay attention.

Otherwise a freak ricochet
could knock your teeth out.

And it was hot back there
concussive, sweat-slippery

a place I'd dream about
for years—an atmosphere

whistling with bombs
as I remember it

grapeshot, cannonballs
all the furious shrapnel

transposed and manifest
of beleaguered adolescence . . .

No wonder we got tired.
There was so much smoke

by the end of the night
we could hardly breath—

we needed air back there
stars in the open hatchway

an icy, offshore gale
crashing on the gun deck . . .

until BANG we were done
the last pin racked

and we found ourselves
taking a leak in fact

out beside the Dumpster
in the literal alley

where it sometimes snowed.
One of us, I remember

had a tattoo. One of us
was missing some teeth.

HOLD IT

Hold it son, my boss would say
hold it right where you are

then came this little lecture
on correct procedure, advice

on how to hold a paintbrush
or mop the flooded restroom.

This was my first job
so I had plenty to learn . . .

How to hold a screwdriver
for instance. Exactly right

precisely so. Light bulbs
weren't so simple either

and sharpening a pencil
was practically impossible.

And yet, despite this close
tedious attention to detail

The Better Letter Service
the only thing he loved

was doomed. Julie, his wife
was an alcoholic for one thing

and for another, the telephones
had all been disconnected . . .

The trade in wedding invitations
invoices, flashy letterheads

evaporated overnight. Pigeons
disremembered flocks of them

were suddenly clamorous all day
under the tattered awnings . . .

Until it just seemed shiftless
not to poison them somehow.

We could burn their bodies
in the trash. Exactly right

precisely so. Our costumes
I remember, entailed goggles

rakes, appropriate brooms—
everything you might expect

by way of promoting correct
total incineration. The dead

however, kept showing up one
by one all winter. The dead

and the almost dead, the ones
who limped around in circles

or fluttered in the icy gutter.
The ones we had to strangle.

Hold it son, my boss would say
hold it right where you are

because a properly wrung neck
was pure technique after all

and the lighting of the pyre
a veritable art. Pushbrooms

matches, everything I touched
bristled with such complexity

I couldn't dream of quitting—
I could barely tie my shoe

and the shock of Julie's breasts
brushing loose along my arm

confused me utterly. *C'mon*
she'd whisper, *don't take things*

so serious. And then a hug.
But what exactly did it mean?

Ambiguous and undulant snow
a powdery, wraithlike mist

sifted down from the gutters
and glittered in the faltering

neon remnant of our sign . . .
Or perhaps another pigeon

limped around in circles
on the sidewalk. Nothing

but this by way of instruction
and nothing for overtime.

HANGING ON LIKE DEATH

The Octopus? The Tilt-a-Whirl?
Whatever it is, it begins

in the twinkling of an eye
to look like so much junk—

but it's too late by then.
By then, the jumpy alcoholic

who collects our tickets
has also strapped us in.

You'd have to be a little kid
to trust this thing. Tools

sinister, odd scraps of metal
scattered in the oily grass . . .

this ride looks absolutely
murderous. "Hang on now"

I tell my daughter. "Hang on."
What else is there to say

when the Octopus has got you?
Or suddenly, some cold, gray morning

a lavender Chevrolet Impala
with different-colored doors

jumps the twisted guardrail
and then comes sliding toward you

sideways, down the interstate.
You'd have to be four years old

and afraid so far of nothing
in this life but monsters

big dogs and snakes to trust
this hanging on, this tilting world

about to vanish, this carnival
we almost missed—and *would* have

except for sheer dumb luck
and the kid who pumped our gas

and answered all our questions
by pointing here and there

along the flickering horizon
with a lit cigarette.

FISHING WITH CHILDREN

Beyond the few clear stumps
and furry sticks, the bottom
drops off quickly, quickly . . .

But it's easy enough to guess
the broken glass and junk
down there, the lost shoes

the stolen bike. Easier
to imagine trash like this
in the gray municipal lagoon

than fish in fact. The four
and five year olds however
keep seeing northern pike—

monster catfish. Even
the worms excite them.
What acrobats they are

especially cut in half!
Urged to bait their own hooks
they stand around staring

at the life in their hands
like so many self-involved
dumbstruck fortune-tellers.

Then they stab themselves
or tangle in the bushes . . .
the whole chaotic business

looking faintly Dionysian
a manic kind of dance almost
or magic stone-age ritual

demanding blood. But later
cast out upon the dark water
our fateful bobbers drift

as over the face of the void
like stars. So we study them
of course, astrologers now

hoping for the smallest sign
or signal of good fortune—
a bluegill, anything at all

from that deep dead calm
where stars and even children
disappear. None of them

for the moment disappearing
though some look tremulous
and on the brink . . .

CREATIVE WRITING

One of my students
has written a story:

it's the end of the world
and an alien spaceship

is circling the planet
trying to make contact.

Hello? Anybody down there?
But it's just as they suspect.

After the atmosphere ignites—
nothing. Not a whimper. Even

our germs are dead. Now
they'll have to start over.

What a drag! Other planets
in the galaxy are doing fine

but you and I, the human race,
we just can't get it somehow.

Perhaps reptiles might work
or something underwater . . .

And so it goes for fifty pages—
fifty million years in fact,

one dimwit, evolutionary dud
after another—until finally

Homo erectus! our old friend
back again. Talk about irony!

The best minds in the universe,
eon upon eon of experiment

and here we are, right back
where we started, doomed—

perfectly ignorant, oblivious
to art, language, metaphor . . .

yet hearing voices nonetheless,
the genius of creation itself

mumbling at us from a cloud.
So what can we do after all

but sweat blood, struggle,
learn to write it down—

never mind the spelling
the printer without ink—

the lords of the universe
are circling the planet

like moths around a desk lamp
and the whole dorm is asleep.

HAMBURGER HEAVEN

A man orders a hamburger
but before he can eat it

he falls off his stool
foaming at the mouth . . .

What is it they tell you
to do with their tongue?

No one, not one customer
in all of Hamburger Heaven

has the foggiest notion.
So maybe the best thing

is to just move over—
give the guy some room.

But this guy is bleeding.
His face is turning blue.

He needs somebody strong
to force open his mouth.

He needs something to bite on
before he breaks his teeth.

His pants are wet. His head
keeps banging on the floor—

on the dumb-fuck cement
of Things-As-They-Are

until finally the loose
feckless white flag

of his Nike flies off
and it's over. Outside

in the slush somewhere
a Salvation Army Santa

rings a faint, faint bell—
but it tastes like blood.

His pants are wet. Then
a blond, ethereal waitress

hands him a shoe—enormous
in his slow comprehension

and heavy as death. Now
he can try to remember

why it was he was born
and the reason for hell

not to mention his name
or the secret of tongues

or what it was exactly
he'd specifically ordered.

ATLANTIS

Stopped for a stoplight
he looks down from an overpass
into a street of little stores—

a party store, cut-rate furniture . . .
stores with boards on the windows
and doorways filled with trash.

Little whirlwinds of cellophane
leaves and paper cups start up—
then a flurry of plastic bags

like jellyfish, go swimming by . . .
as if he were looking down
from inside a submarine perhaps

at some ancient, weed-dense city—
some lost and blear Atlantis
stirring eerily to life again

under the piss-colored light
of his sodium lamps. Old stoves
toilets, some burned-up cars . . .

piles and troves like these
fill whole backyards down there—
bedsprings, washing machines

a bathtub full of bricks . . .
as if, in the last days,
collecting junk like this

became a form of prayer. Then
the light turns green again
and he's back on the interstate

listening to the news. Something
about "Humanitarian Aid." Contras
Russian tanks in Nicaragua . . .

but his mind is somewhere else.
In the cold, atavistic muck
just behind him in the dark

something big has been disturbed—
a giant eel, a rope of mucus
the steady coiling and uncoiling

of a wormlike, blind indifference
that feeds upon the drowned
the poor too poor to withstand

the first, least wave of unemployment
the smallest kind of war
children buried in the rubble

dragonflies, like gunships,
hovering over some putrescence
on the weedy shore.

Tall Birds Stalking (1994)

ADIOS ZARATHUSTRA

They were watching it
for a niece who watched
their dog last summer:

a geriatric cockatoo
named Zarathustra

who could ride a scooter
talk dirty, and sometimes
properly coaxed, squawk

a few strangled bars
of the "Star Spangled Banner."

It also loved mirrors
bright dangly earrings
and being out of its cage—

like a privileged trustee
they thought, some harmless

old lifer who had learned
long since, that Alcatraz
was Alcatraz—inescapable

and the only home he had.
Where could he want to go?

But when he saw his chance
when they let the dog out once
it was adios Zarathustra—

gone: a small white hanky
waving from the lilacs . . .

they posted notices of course
which likewise disappeared—
Buddhistic little prayers

fluttering in the Laundromat
gas station, grocery store . . .

until finally it was winter
and dark by five o'clock . . .
Nothing could save him now.

Which eschatological fact
their niece, a young woman

in her twenties, engaged
and just back from Europe
could accept with a shrug.

Why get all worked up? An old
mean-tempered bird like that . . .

While they, on the other hand,
wrestling his cage back down
from its vain, crabapple bower

were depressed by his mirrors
and earrings for months . . .

And they had other feelings too—
curious, heartbreaking dreams
they were ashamed, at first

to confess. Love dreams
involving different people

from as far back as college—
everyone they had ever liked
or gone to bed with it seemed—

some of them dead by now
some of them still beautiful

lost out there in the snow
in the land of the free
the home of the brave.

THE AWARDS BANQUET

1. What Kind of Poetry Do You Write?

The university was thriving—
one of the best in the world
and getting better . . .

Absolutely the place to be
if you were interested at all
in superconductivity
electromagnetic imaging
or biodegradable plastics . . .

And who wasn't after all?

We were just sitting down to eat
reading each other's name tags
introducing ourselves . . . Then

by way of breaking the ice
an international genius
in high-speed computing
takes notice of the poet:

Well, so you're the poet . . .

As if I were painted blue
and wore a bone in my nose.

Next he wants to know
what kind of poetry I write—

because of course he's guessed
there must be different kinds
just as there are different kinds
of astronomy or physics . . .

When I say I write free verse
and rely for the most part
on my own experience

the whole table gets suddenly
busy with their salads.

They understand perfectly.
They wouldn't read that stuff
at gunpoint. Why should they?

They're too busy prying apart
the atom, splicing genes
planning trips to Mars
Jupiter, Alpha Centauri . . .

Besides that
no one writes in meter
and nothing rhymes anymore.

2. *Squash Soup*

Halfway through the squash soup
there's a disturbance . . . shouts

a loud clattering of dishes
from the chancellor's table . . .

then two campus policemen
dragging someone to the door.

The "lunatic" it turns out.
The guy in the baseball cap

who almost ruined everything—
the robotics seminar, the talk

on artificial intelligence . . .
even the poetry reading:

a hallucination almost—
there, in the front row

tight-lipped, spit whitening
the corners of his mouth

his eyes too antic-bright
his whole aspect jittery

with manic calculation . . .
until he's finally up

and shouting *Liar! Filth!*
followed by certain verses

from the Bible. God knows
what he's told the chancellor

fussing dimly with his tie . . .
A little squash soup perhaps.

Nothing really. Not blood.
Not a bullet hole at least.

And now he's even smiling.
A lunatic for Christ's sake.

What's the world coming to?
my neighbor wants to know

winking at the lovely chemist.
Tell us. You're the poet.

Meanwhile, at another table
Prometheus whispers something

to the inventor of the wheel—
then draws it on a napkin.

3. *Speech*

After dessert, it's time
for the great hall to fall silent
and face the dais.

Now the chancellor
and the vice chancellor
shall deliver their odes.

And at the sound of the ox horn
let the heroes approach
and bear off their trophies . . .

Everyone but the poet that is
who keeps falling asleep, then
snorting suddenly awake again

like one of those clever
little birds on springs
that attach to drinking glasses—

a gift, something his father
of whom he now fitfully dreams
as a matter of fact

has just brought him home
from the bar. It's winter
and there's frost on the windows.

It's after supper; a sudden
clattering of dishes, shouts . . .
and through it all the bird

bobs down and drinks over
and over from the still water
of the white kitchen table

miraculous as human speech—
a baby saying *Bird! Bird!*
there, in the black window.

IN THE CHARIOT DRAWN
BY DRAGONS

Such a chariot has Helios, my father's father,
Given to me to defend me from my enemies.
   —Euripedes, *Medea*

Fascinating the way our dreams
accommodate the muddled here

and now—the phone we answer
in our sleep for instance
before it startles us awake

or just this morning, the cat
killing something in the yard—

a baby rabbit it turns out
squealing that one high note
only nightmares comprehend . . .

the one where real children
lie dismembered in their beds—

as, indeed, I heard it spoken
on the evening news . . . Medea
of course, was never mentioned

although I understood at once
the way we often do in dreams

that it was she again—disguised
in this last, horrific incarnation
to look like almost anyone . . .

a forgotten second cousin say
whose husband studied neutron

stars, black holes . . . matters
so quantum mechanically intense
so distant, it would take her

nearly fifteen billion years
of living practically abandoned

in married student housing
with two frenetic, infant sons
and no help at all from anyone

before she understood at last
that everything was hopeless—

that nothing, not even light
not the merest glimmer of it
could ever escape such gravity—

a force so crushing in the end
she could barely lift the knife

and wake us up again, heart
pounding, to some poor rabbit
screaming as the sun comes up

or Medea in her bloody bathrobe
and the chariot drawn by dragons.

CRAWLSPACE

In coastal Florida
where my mother lives

the old are everywhere
but some feel younger

by the minute. *Terrific!*
Never better! my mother's

diabetic neighbor shouts
from her tipsy lawn tractor.

I'm like a kid down here!
Everyday vicissitude however

that water-dance of local light
partakes of something different

something ancient and Egyptian—
like red tides, for instance

or those nightmare catfish
that walk around like lizards.

That's why, playing pinochle
our conversation turns to snakes—

a recent python in particular
all twenty-one feet of it

police and zoo officials
have to extricate by hand

from the feculent crawlspace
beneath the yacht-club restaurant.

There's even a picture of it
in the paper: *Long Lost Pet*

Found at Last . . . but nervous
and with an appetite for dogs.

Then it's time to have a drink
and consider citrus canker

or mothlike flakes of snow
that kill the oranges overnight.

We're all like kids down here . . .
our fathers, our lovely mothers

having all gone off somewhere
leaving us alone and listening

to something awful moving
in the leaves beneath the house.

LATE

The dog begs to go out
then whines immediately
to come back in again.

It must be 25 below . . .
a fine snow sifts down
from off the roof somewhere

glittering, alive almost . . .
a blizzard of tiny fish
or phosphorescent plankton

all hypnotized no doubt
by the backdoor porch light.
The crabapple, the lilacs

so still, so intricate
look likewise submarine—
rare black corals maybe

or arborescent lesions
deep within the brain . . .
It's after six o'clock.

And on the next block
at some impossible depth
where imagination falters

an ordinary snow shovel
scrapes its way along
through frozen drifts

of tiny skeletons, muck,
blind, anaerobic worms—
charm bracelets, shoes

the dead, literal snow
where the world escapes
its proper metaphor

and one's only child
simply misses her supper
forever and ever.

TALL BIRDS STALKING

1. The Moon over the AMOCO Sign

That long first day
after fifteen hours

of Illinois, Kentucky
Tennessee and Georgia

any vacancy would do—
a barn, a chicken coop . . .

but we drove on forever
until we came to Heaven

our daughter's dream
come true, a real motel

complete with water slide
and *Jaws* on HBO. Three

or four drinks later
relaxed, half-paralyzed

on our little balcony
I watch the full moon

the merest apparition
a mirage of some kind

float improbably up
from behind a Pizza Hut

then turn completely real
just above the AMOCO sign

on the bypass heading south
where my father was dying . . .

Gangrene again. Another leg.
This time above the knee.

Inside our flickering room
my daughter's movie screams

and screams. Tomorrow
when we get to the gulf

she'll be afraid to swim—
imagining the bloody water

dismembered arms and legs
the endless, true abyss

where an ordinary moon
was shining, even now.

2. *What's My Name?*

Strange machines
have landed on the roof
outside my father's window . . .

and so my mother sighs
pulls down the shade

and starts asking questions:

What's my name?
she wants to know.
Who am I? Whereupon

confused, frightened
by all this urgency

flower-feathered birds
that live on morphine
flutter in the curtains.

There! my father points.
There! as if the room
were really full of names

flying frantically about
looking for a place to land . . .

but they're only birds
and quite as nameless

as the air conditioner
taking off again, rising
out there on the roof

like Charon's helicopter
or some terrible angel
from the Apocalypse . . .

Meanwhile, his black
altogether anonymous foot
is resting on its pillow.

Another face almost—
wide awake, monstrous

to which, all afternoon
our helpless eyes advert

as if we'd heard it cough
clear its throat a little

and even try to speak.

3. Tall Birds Stalking

Dawn. On the horizon
a single mushroom cloud

has grown up overnight
from the jade-green gulf
like a real mushroom . . .

but because it is not
the end of the world

but only Tuesday, Monday
or maybe Wednesday . . . the day
anyway, after the delivery

of his father's small ashes
from the Cremation Society

a grown man and his mother
are walking on the beach
discussing life insurance.

Arguing in the air above them
the usual flock of innocuous birds . . .

And then, up ahead, a fisherman
casting from the stone jetty
strikes a fish, a giant snook

or shark or even barracuda
that takes out all his line.

The grown man and his mother
the retired couple collecting
shark teeth—all of them

stop dead in their tracks.
This is interesting. This

reminds them of something
dangerous: a fall perhaps
down icy steps, a stroke . . .

and then that final, headlong
acceleration of the spirit

out among the galaxies—
the cold, starry ocean
where it feels at home . . .

A tall, blue-gray heron
another rock until now

stabs a piece of lost bait
from a crevice. The fisherman
sits down tired on his bucket

and the grown man, everyone,
knows just how he feels

having been there before
in that hieroglyphic of grief
with tall birds stalking.

UNCOMFORTABLE PROCEDURES

January 1991

January, the first of six
"uncomfortable procedures"

as my periodontist puts it
putting down his scissors

with a stoic little sigh
among the tinkling knives

still trembling on my chest.
"But let's try this," he says

loading up a fresh syringe
"let's try to get this right."

And then he disappears again
to phone his nurse, Jolene

who isn't here this morning
because her car won't start.

My doctor's clinic of course
is in the middle of nowhere

way out by Oakwood Estates
where no one even lives—

nor are there any sidewalks yet
or trees. From where I sit

waiting for my face to freeze
it's all just broken stalks

of trembling corn out there
buckets, shingles—misery

sufficient unto the day thereof
or any part that I can see

for all that blowing snow . . .
So when Jolene arrives (sorry

sorry that she's late again)
by Yellow Cab from far Rantoul

it seems a kind of miracle . . .
But it's clear she's had it—

a husband in the Air Force
two kids in nursery school

"and now yesterday," she says
"they go and start a goddamn war."

To which the good doctor replies:
"Can I please, if you don't mind

have a little more suction here?"
He wants to get things right.

And who knows how the null abyss
might look—the war, my mouth

all those fields out there—
once the condominiums go up

and they put a golf course in?
The thing to do is be precise—

as in precision bombing say
or surgical strikes . . . mere

uncomfortable procedures really
and over before you know it.

The Last Neanderthal (1999)

CLARITY

We rented our vacation cottage
every summer of my childhood
from the same glum farmer—

a giant, cadaverous Chippewa
with ten children, who never
seemed to look at us at all.

We paid the rent, picked up
the oars for our rowboat
then drove uncertainly off

through his dolorous chickens
to whatever slapdash hovel
matched the number on our oars.

No running water, no electricity
and no gas either that I remember.
A wood stove maybe, an outhouse

but inevitably a place so small
and flimsy, so chipped or bent
in each detail, it seemed to us

just charming, doll-like really—
as if it might have been a diorama
in some museum of natural history.

Except that starting now of course
we'd have to live there. Hornets
bats, the snake in the cupboard . . .

Take it easy, mother said. *Relax.*
She was born and raised up here
when northern Michigan was still

a dream-time, howling wilderness
of cold starvation and diphtheria.
She'd chop that snake to pieces.

And then she'd tuck me into a bed
exactly like the one she slept in
as a child. Every night, the same

huge shadows on the walls, the same
crickets, owls, and scrambling mice . . .
until once I even dreamt till dawn

that I could hear her baby sister
coughing. They gave her turpentine
I think, with lots of sugar in it

but she died anyway. That's why
at first light, there was so much
fog on the black water. No one

was up yet. Under our green boat
pulled halfway up on the beach
where the giant boatman left it

I found a brilliant leopard frog
beside a tiny, coal-black bullhead.
How still, how exquisite they look

even now, after all these years . . .
having achieved, in the mind's eye
the perfect clarity of last things.

THE ELEPHANT IN WINTER

During the winter of course
they kept the elephant inside.

His "house," or dungeon really
was practically hidden by brush

and backed up to a small canal
just off the intricate main canal

behind Detroit's Belle Isle zoo
on which you could skate for miles—

forever, if you happened to forget
in a rattling wind beyond surmise

or earshot of the lost pavilion
just which way you'd come exactly

now that all the trees were dark—
the footbridge wrong completely . . .

And it's right about here, in little
thudding intervals at first, I felt

the ice begin to move. Okay, sure
I thought: snow trucks. The muffled

banging of some inscrutable pump
or boiler maybe . . . until, apropos

of nothing but that, a full-grown
male elephant goes suddenly berserk

a scant ten feet away, the whole
five-ton, concussive bulk of him

exploding into high-pitched screams
and a scattering of creeper twigs

every time he throws himself, KA-BOOM!
against the icy wall he lived behind.

That much at least is crystal clear.
But afterward . . . I don't know. Perhaps

I fainted or went into shock somehow—
only to be rescued later by wolves . . .

Or maybe my father showed up finally
blinking his tiny, puzzled headlights

right where he was supposed to meet me
a good two hours ago with the car . . .

But isn't that the way with children?
Things that must have truly happened

end up blurred, inextricably confused
with dreams—so that, years later

a prized inheritance, a china cabinet
tinkling with the dishes and crystal

my mother only used at Christmas
eerily recalls, as much as anything

that dreamlike moment on the ice . . .
or the labyrinth, in fact, of home itself—

the angry stirring of the Minotaur
whom I've just woken up somehow

and now, by Christ, he's had enough—
whose least footstep shakes the house.

PERISCOPE

Waiting for sleep
and aimlessly adrift
on the wine-lulled sea

of late middle age—
my own dark ship

rising and falling
in undulant doldrum
on the bibulous deep—

I find that often now
I've drifted back to 1958

and the South China Sea
where I'm nineteen again . . .
a yawning midwatch lookout

on the USS *Regulus*, AF 57—
a tublike refrigeration ship

Joseph Conrad would have loved
right down to the dull romance
of being repeatedly torpedoed

by any friendly submarine
that needed target practice.

But for my part, I preferred
just sort of looking around
through my feckless binoculars

at all the unguessable stars
of the Malay Archipelago.

Recklessly adrift one minute
with everything there was
to do or dream or be, then

lost again as merest plankton
amid the dangerous menagerie

of the southern constellations,
it's no wonder on occasion
a sudden phosphorescent torpedo

off our port or starboard bow
escaped my notice entirely . . .

but for those keeping score
of course, sending our ship
theoretically to the bottom.

*Holy jumping Christ! Send that
asshole up here on the double!*

And yet, after all these years
those same stars and meteors
even the squat *Regulus* herself

rolling along at fourteen knots
in fat silhouette on the horizon

still appear to me sometimes
before sleep, in perfect focus—
but slightly magnified too

and just a little tilted maybe
as if I were in a wave trough

or otherwise below the horizon
and looking out from that angle
through my binoculars again—

or, more oddly still
through a periscope somehow . . .

There she is: her cargo masts
and hopeless three-inch guns—
her lookout talking to himself

singing . . . Is he allowed to smoke?
How young he looks! How innocent!

And how swiftly as the years
are those torpedoes streaking
toward him, fore and aft.

BEAUTY

There is nothing so beautiful as that which does not exist.

  —Paul Valéry, *The Art of Poetry*

After I got out of the Navy
I loafed at home for a while
then enrolled myself in college . . .

I wanted to make something of myself—
become an accountant like my cousin

or, sweet Jesus, a lawyer. But somehow
(who knows what happens to our dreams?)
I found myself writing poems instead.

I was taking a class in poetry writing
and wrote whenever I could—all night

after my job loading trucks sometimes
at a card table down in the basement . . .
But when the sun came up, how odd

how astonishing it was, to realize
that time had simply disappeared!

And there, in front of me, timeless
for all I knew, the night-born poem:
"Seabent," I remember one beginning

"with slowly beating wings
the sunwashed seabirds pass . . ."

Reading it out loud made me dizzy
and I carried it around in my pocket
for days—although, at the same time

what I really felt soared impatiently
beyond words somehow. "Sunwashed

seabirds?" What kind were they exactly?
And where in that truck-loading life
had I stood enthralled to watch them?

Some snot-beaked, garbage-eating gulls
down by the Detroit River maybe . . .

Or, in the Navy, those creaky albatross
I'd tossed Tabasco-sauced bread to
from the fantail of our ship. Mindless

and cruel, beauty was the last thing
I think I would have ever thought of.

So why was I thinking of it now
and staying up all night to find it?
Whatever it was that made the hair

on the back of my arms stand up
and that darkness in the window

in the merest blinking of an eye
to somehow disappear—leaving me
at a card table in an old coal bin

with one bare bulb hanging down . . .
I can remember thinking, even then

how it could have been a jail cell
a room where prisoners were tortured
the last place on God's grim earth

where poetry might happen. And yet
now and then, rising up from nowhere

on slowly beating wings, something—
I knew there was something, born
perhaps of the heart's pure yearning

that would save my life: Beauty
the name for those birds was Beauty.

TWILIGHT OF THE NEANDERTHALS

1. Fog

The rain has finally stopped
and now a cold fog has settled
over the burned-out forest
where we have come to gather

firewood, I think . . . or maybe
berries of some kind.

                Up ahead
I can hear the dangerous water
rushing loudly over stones . . .

and beyond that, crows again
arguing our intentions here—
which are not clear,
                not clear . . .

being one more instance merely
of an inveterate forgetfulness
for which we have no adequate
language,
          only the monosyllabic
smell of ashes and scorched trees—

the acrid, pungent grammar
of the afternoon itself,
                    the dead
dendritic thickets of some lost
connection here . . .
                    wherein
bereft alike of sunlight, syntax
or even brute analogy, we stumble
from one amnesia to another . . .

unable to distinguish finally
between mastodons made entirely
of fog
          and the real catastrophe.

2. *Arithmetic*

How is it
          that we never learned
to count?
          How is it, nonetheless
that some of us seem always
to be missing?

                    I remember
watching a mother duck once
swimming in a weedy estuary
with her babies . . . then
                    half-asleep
being startled by a loud splash—
sploosh! as if someone had thrown
a rock in the water—
                    followed

by a quacking, two-second flurry
of duck-motherly consternation . . .

which meant that one of them
was missing of course,
                    or even
more . . . But on the other hand
without being able to count
how could she ever be sure?

and so she sensibly
                    forgets it
and preens herself instead—
reassured, calmed in an instant
by the lively,
                    hysterical peeping
of those who were spared . . .

curiously unlike ourselves
for whom the dead are never
simply absent,
                    but experienced
rather more the way old hunters
feel pain for years sometimes
in a chewed-off arm or leg.

Or suppose this very afternoon
near the riverbank
                    in the fog
we heard the sound of something
heavy falling into water . . .
                              then
screams,
          indicating one of us—
who also never learned to swim.

Ridiculous to think it doesn't
make a difference
                    beyond all number.

And besides,
            we have the body
which must be buried with masses
of flowers, masses of flowers . . .

or left for the animals.

3. *Cro-Magnons*

Friends they say,
                    cousins even
who come to us from the south
with tools and valuable skills . . .

When game is scarce,
                    they know
how to set the forest on fire
and where to wait in ambush

for whatever squealing thing
half-cooked
                    and barely alive
they can kill with a stick . . .

And sometimes they have dreams
that tell them
                    where the swift
uncatchable horses are grazing—
aurochs and great woolly mammoths

they drive by the herd
                    over cliffs
killing them all—
                    until finally
they've even terrified themselves

and thus must ask forgiveness
of the dead—
                    recreating them
by torchlight
                    in bright ochre
on the walls of our mutual cave . . .

or, as happens more
                    and more
frequently of late,
                    in rooms
far, far back in the labyrinth
where we are not allowed—

rooms echoing with high-pitched
little bone whistles,
                    drums
screams they refuse to explain . . .

although afterward
                    some of us
seem always to be missing.

Caught in the open
                    they'll say
by a bungled grass fire.
                    Lost

on the glacier,
                    buried forever
in the avalanche . . .
                              accidents
only they have witnessed.

And no doubt because our grief
annoys them,
                    we are sometimes
given strange, medicinal herbs
to help us forget—
                              potions
engendering uncomfortable dreams—

dreams of walking through fog
dreams of the burned-out forest . . .

and lately,
                    recurring dreams
of food . . .
                    or rather,
                              bones merely—

belonging to some delicious animal
we can't remember eating,
                              of course.

GHOST

Coming in from the morning's run
sweaty but not tired, feeling better
really, than I have for years

adolescent, even, in my specific
and innocent thirst for orange juice
after three whole weeks of not drinking

I catch, just barely audible at first
over the cold hum of the refrigerator
an arrhythmic, suspicious fluttering

from down in the basement somewhere—
a frayed belt on the washing machine
a part working loose in the dryer . . .

followed by the unmistakable thump
of something soft hitting a window—
something alive and fluttering again

in the ductwork above the furnace . . .
a bird of course. A starling finally
dragging a huge, claw-footed shadow

from window to window, wrestling it
from pipe to flue, croaking a little
in his terror, like one of the damned

who, having fallen in this instance
down the black hole of our chimney
finds himself floundering in the gloom

of another whole universe entirely—
an underworld of gray cement in fact
redolent of mildew, old laundry, dreams

in which I keep hearing tiny noises
and then find my dead brother again
hiding in the furnace with a shotgun.

Just now, however, in this wide-awake
absolutely sober, forty-watt flashback
of the actual suicide basement, he seems

to be a bird. As a child, I remember
he was always jumping off of things—
couches, porch rails, the garage roof . . .

So perhaps it's perfectly natural now
for him to be a bird, confused like this
with no memory at all of the old life—

neither the porch, nor the rose of Sharon
he sailed right over in his wash-towel cape.
Not his mother, not his father passed out

snoring on the swing. And not me certainly
watching my brother as he asked me to—
drinking my juice at the top of our steps.

SHANGRI-LA

By ten o'clock the snow
has stopped and a west wind
has pushed the clouds apart

exposing little bits of sky
like ponds of windswept ice

where now and then Orion
or some other constellation
drifts partly into view . . .

No traffic. No sounds at all
except the dog, snuffling along

delirious, through the powdery
chest-deep snow of Shangri-la
for all she knows . . . And then

quick as a rabbit, the moon
breaks free again, followed

closely by a star—the merest
tooth or lynx-bright eye perhaps
of something still ineffable—

cruel as the gravity in dreams
of running nowhere in deep snow . . .

But for one skipped heartbeat
with clouds in sudden wisps
like underwater blood almost

swirling darkly out behind them
how fast they both seem moving!

An illusion so convincing, even
the dog takes notice—barking
furiously, every hair electric

the way she barks each morning
at mostly phantom garbage men

or birds, the very light itself—
some world she still remembers
from fifty million years ago . . .

A feeling I'll share tomorrow
reading the paper at breakfast

in the busy student union—
the talk around me adolescent
suburban in its accent

and focused mainly on the weather
like all the front-page pictures

in the paper: stranded motorists
buried cars . . . then, on page two
a photograph that seems at first

to be a shot of absolutely nothing—
a blank hillside of trampled snow

that turns out to be a creek bank
in that very park we walked through—
a weedless slope some homeless drunk

had tumbled down, over and over
again, invisibly drowning finally

without a name, at the bottom
of the page—my dog still barking
for all I know. How strange

listening to the talk around me
so feckless, so immortal really

to think he might have heard her
and seen the naked moon like that
swiftly, swiftly going nowhere.

IN THE COMPANY OF MANATEES

The samurai looks insignificant
beside his armor of black dragon scales.

   —Tomas Transtromer, "After a Death"

One by one, every ten minutes
or so by my watch, the manatees
at the Tampa zoo float slowly up

like tiny, one-man subs for air . . .
and then, their dive tanks flooding
to a delicate, negative buoyancy

sink, at one-half foot per second
to just within their body's width
of bottom—no longer submarines

at all, but stumps of driftwood
sea wrack now, without one hint
of sentience or least volition . . .

unless, of course, one counts
at the foggy observation window
all their several amputations

and propeller scars—evidence
that might just point to something
darkly headlong in their nature

or warlike and ferocious even . . .
until they look like samurai almost—
but dazed, adrift in shock somehow

lost in the dreamy aftermath perhaps
of some great slaughter. What mercies
might their enemies expect after all

face to face with these grim veterans—
so calm, so *still* in their nicked-up
criss-crossed, black dragon armor!

Otherwise, that thumping roar outside
is probably not an air raid, artillery
or ski boats blowing up in Tampa harbor

but rather, an ordinary bulldozer
clearing ground for a new addition—
another wing for the gravely wounded

like the one who floats above me now
eating lettuce in a corner, her tail
lopped and short a starboard flipper.

A civilian obviously. An orphaned
adolescent, no larger than my daughter
who keeps on looking at her watch, bored

and grounded here with her dim parents
all afternoon between planes, a hurricane
still threatening in the aviary palms . . .

She'd rather be skiing, of course—
at dusk, among the dangerous mangroves.
She's thinking, I know, of the smooth

black water, the way it feels, her skis
chattering over it for miles and miles . . .
She can't stand this sitting still.

Nor has she ever seen those clouds
of sudden blood that sometimes blossom
close behind us in this headlong life.

Her own sweet limbs and spirit still
intact, her own bad dreams just dreams,
how can I explain what keeps me here

among these submarines and samurai
these poor, maimed beasts come back
. . . from where? In all their terrible

unforgiving innocence.

THE LAST NEANDERTHAL

Browsing in the waiting room
through dog-eared TIME, he reads
how all over the world, frogs

are disappearing—a thinning
it's supposed, of the ozone . . .

and then it's his turn. Blood
pressure, prostate palpation . . .
followed by the usual questions:

Any . . . um . . . trouble getting it up?
Painful or bloody urination?

Not so far. But one day, he thinks
it could all be different. The light
becoming suddenly brighter, ominous

and the doctor frowning meanwhile
snapping off his rubber gloves . . .

After that, surgery, chemotherapy
the rest of his life in diapers . . .
But for now, except for a niggling

slight elevation in blood pressure
he's OK and deserves a handshake:

Keep up the good work. Exercise.
And take this form to the front desk.
We need your group insurance number.

And soon he's driving home again
curiously aware of the littered

roadside, the look of late March—
blossoms of Styrofoam and paper cups
shivering in the stiff, brown bushes

while overhead drift clouds of lead—
a sky that might rain anything:

dead dogs and cats for instance—
car junk, disemboweled sofas . . . even
the radio stinks. Continual static

interrupting a talk show of some kind.
Some paleoanthropologist it seems

talking about our human origins—
and people calling in with questions:
What about those Neanderthals then?

Were they human or not? And why
if they were as smart as you seem

to think, did they all die out?
OK I'll hang up now and listen.
At which point, the station disappears

and there's nothing on the air again
but noise, a sound like leaves perhaps

rattling in an empty cave somewhere
along the Rhine . . . It's almost dark.
Nearby, the last Neanderthal hunkers

over a small fire, roasting a frog
on a stick. A man much like himself

but bigger and covered with hair—
his low forehead wrinkled suddenly
by something he hears out there . . .

a car whizzing by in another dimension.
It's possible. If he can imagine it

why not? Meanwhile, the frog
looks almost done. A small frog
the size of a baseball or an enlarged

prostate maybe. He can see it clearly.
A middle-aged man much like himself.

Michael Van Walleghen received his bachelor
of arts degree in English from Wayne State
University in Detroit and his master of fine
arts in creative writing from the University of
Iowa. He is he author of five previous books
of poetry: *The Wichita Poems* (1975); *More
Trouble with the Obvious* (1981), winner of
the 1980 Lamont Poetry Prize of the Academy
of American Poets; *Blue Tango* (1989); *Tall
Birds Stalkings* (1994); and *The Last Neander-
thal* (1999). Van Walleghen is a professor of
English at the University of Illinois Urbana-
Champaign.

Illinois Poetry Series

Laurence Lieberman, Editor

In It
Stephen Berg (1986)

The Ghosts of Who We Were
Phyllis Thompson (1986)

Moon in a Mason Jar
Robert Wrigley (1986)

Lower-Class Heresy
T. R. Hummer (1987)

Poems: New and Selected
Frederick Morgan (1987)

Furnace Harbor: A Rhapsody of the
North Country
Philip D. Church (1988)

Bad Girl, with Hawk
Nance Van Winckel (1988)

Blue Tango
Michael Van Walleghen (1989)

Eden
Dennis Schmitz (1989)

Waiting for Poppa at the Smithtown
Diner
Peter Serchuk (1990)

Great Blue
Brendan Galvin (1990)

What My Father Believed
Robert Wrigley (1991)

Something Grazes Our Hair
S. J. Marks (1991)

Walking the Blind Dog
G. E. Murray (1992)

The Sawdust War
Jim Barnes (1992)

The God of Indeterminacy
Sandra McPherson (1993)

Off-Season at the Edge of the World
Debora Greger (1994)

Counting the Black Angels
Len Roberts (1994)

Oblivion
Stephen Berg (1995)

To Us, All Flowers Are Roses
Lorna Goodison (1995)

Honorable Amendments
Michael S. Harper (1995)

Points of Departure
Miller Williams (1995)

Dance Script with Electric Ballerina
Alice Fulton (reissue, 1996)

To the Bone: New and Selected
Poems
Sydney Lea (1996)

Floating on Solitude
Dave Smith (3-volume reissue, 1996)

Bruised Paradise
Kevin Stein (1996)

Walt Whitman Bathing
David Wagoner (1996)

Rough Cut
Thomas Swiss (1997)

Paris
Jim Barnes (1997)

The Ways We Touch
Miller Williams (1997)

The Rooster Mask
Henry Hart (1998)

The Trouble-Making Finch
Len Roberts (1998)

Grazing
Ira Sadoff (1998)

Turn Thanks
Lorna Goodison (1999)

Traveling Light:
Collected and New Poems
David Wagoner (1999)

Some Jazz a While:
Collected Poems
Miller Williams (1999)

The Iron City
John Bensko (2000)

Songlines in Michaeltree: New and
Collected Poems
Michael S. Harper (2000)

Pursuit of a Wound
Sydney Lea (2000)

The Pebble: Old and New Poems
Mairi MacInnes (2000)

Chance Ransom
Kevin Stein (2000)

House of Poured-Out Waters
Jane Mead (2001)

The Silent Singer: New and Selected
Poems
Len Roberts (2001)

The Salt Hour
J. P. White (2001)

Guide to the Blue Tongue
Virgil Suárez (2002)

The House of Song
David Wagoner (2002)

X =
Stephen Berg (2002)

Arts of a Cold Sun
G. E. Murray (2003)

Barter
Ira Sadoff (2003)

The Hollow Log Lounge
R. T. Smith (2003)

In the Black Window: New and
Selected Poems
Michael Van Walleghen (2004)

National Poetry Series

Eroding Witness
Nathaniel Mackey (1985)
Selected by Michael S. Harper

Palladium
Alice Fulton (1986)
Selected by Mark Strand

Cities in Motion
Sylvia Moss (1987)
Selected by Derek Walcott

The Hand of God and a Few Bright
Flowers
William Olsen (1988)
Selected by David Wagoner

The Great Bird of Love
Paul Zimmer (1989)
Selected by William Stafford

Stubborn
Roland Flint (1990)
Selected by Dave Smith

The Surface
Laura Mullen (1991)
Selected by C. K. Williams

The Dig
Lynn Emanuel (1992)
Selected by Gerald Stern

My Alexandria
Mark Doty (1993)
Selected by Philip Levine

The High Road to Taos
Martin Edmunds (1994)
Selected by Donald Hall

Theater of Animals
Samn Stockwell (1995)
Selected by Louise Glück

The Broken World
Marcus Cafagña (1996)
Selected by Yusef Komunyakaa

Nine Skies
A. V. Christie (1997)
Selected by Sandra McPherson

Lost Wax
Heather Ramsdell (1998)
Selected by James Tate

So Often the Pitcher Goes to Water
until It Breaks
Rigoberto González (1999)
Selected by Ai

Renunciation
Corey Marks (2000)
Selected by Philip Levine

Manderley
Rebecca Wolff (2001)
Selected by Robert Pinsky

Theory of Devolution
David Groff (2002)
Selected by Mark Doty

Rhythm and Booze
Julie Kane (2003)
Selected by Maxine Kumin

Other Poetry Volumes

Local Men and *Domains*
James Whitehead (1987)

Her Soul beneath the Bone: Women's
Poetry on Breast Cancer
Edited by Leatrice Lifshitz (1988)

Days from a Dream Almanac
Dennis Tedlock (1990)

Working Classics: Poems on
Industrial Life
*Edited by Peter Oresick and
Nicholas Coles* (1990)

Hummers, Knucklers, and Slow
Curves: Contemporary Baseball
Poems
Edited by Don Johnson (1991)

The Double Reckoning of
Christopher Columbus
Barbara Helfgott Hyett (1992)

Selected Poems
Jean Garrigue (1992)

New and Selected Poems, 1962–92
Laurence Lieberman (1993)

The Dig and *Hotel Fiesta*
Lynn Emanuel (1994)

For a Living: The Poetry of Work
*Edited by Nicholas Coles and Peter
Oresick* (1995)

The Tracks We Leave: Poems on
Endangered Wildlife of North
America
Barbara Helfgott Hyett (1996)

Peasants Wake for Fellini's *Casanova*
and Other Poems
*Andrea Zanzotto; edited and
translated by John P. Welle and
Ruth Feldman; drawings by
Federico Fellini and Augusto
Murer* (1997)

Moon in a Mason Jar and *What My
Father Believed*
Robert Wrigley (1997)

The Wild Card: Selected Poems,
  Early and Late
*Karl Shapiro; edited by Stanley
  Kunitz and David Ignatow* (1998)

Turtle, Swan and *Bethlehem in
  Broad Daylight*
Mark Doty (2000)

Illinois Voices: An Anthology of
  Twentieth-Century Poetry
*Edited by Kevin Stein and G. E.
  Murray* (2001)

On a Wing of the Sun
Jim Barnes (3-volume reissue, 2001)

Poems
*William Carlos Williams;
  introduction by Virginia M.
  Wright-Peterson* (2002)

Creole Echoes: The Francophone
  Poetry of Nineteenth-Century
  Louisiana
*Translated by Norman R. Shapiro;
  introduction and notes by M. Lynn
  Weiss* (2003)

Poetry from *Sojourner:* A Feminist
  Anthology
*Edited by Ruth Lepson with Lynne
  Yamaguchi; introduction by Mary
  Loeffelholz* (2003)

Asian American Poetry: The Next
  Generation
*Edited by Victoria M. Chang;
  foreword by Marilyn Chin* (2004)

The University of Illinois Press
is a founding member of the
Association of American University Presses.

———————————————————

Composed in 10/13 Sabon
with Franklin Gothic display
by Jim Proefrock
at the University of Illinois Press
Designed by Paula Newcomb
Manufactured by Sheridan Books, Inc.

University of Illinois Press
1325 South Oak Street
Champaign, IL 61820-6903
www.press.uillinois.edu